World Book's Human Body Works

The Digestive System
The Urinary System

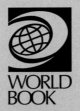

WORLD
BOOK

a Scott Fetzer company
Chicago

www.worldbookonline.com

World Book, Inc.
233 N. Michigan Ave.
Chicago, IL 60601 U.S.A.

For information about other World Book publications, visit our Web site at **http://www.worldbook.com** or call **1-800-WORLDBK (967-5325)**. For information about sales to schools and libraries, call **1-800-975-3250 (United States); 1-800-837-5365 (Canada).**

World Book, Inc.
Editor in Chief: Paul A. Kobasa
Managing Editor: Maureen Mostyn Licbenson
Graphics and Design Manager: Sandra M. Dyrlund
Research Services Manager: Loranne K. Shields
Permissions Editor: Janet T. Peterson

Library of Congress Cataloging-in-Publication Data
The digestive system/the urinary system.
     p. cm. -- (World Book's human body works)
  Includes bibliographical references and index.
  ISBN-13: 978-0-7166-4429-3
  ISBN-10: 0-7166-4429-0
  1. Digestive organs--Juvenile literature. 2. Urinary organs--Juvenile literature. 3. Digestion--Juvenile literature.
I. World Book, Inc. II. Series.
  QP145.D569 2006
  612.3--dc22
                               2005034768

World Book's Human Body Works (set)
ISBN 13: 978-0-7166-4425-5
ISBN 10: 0-7166-4425-8

Printed in China

07 08 09 10 5 4 3

Product development: Arcturus Publishing Limited
Writer: Chris Oxlade
Editor: Alex Woolf
Designer: Jane Hawkins

Acknowledgments
Corbis: cover (Michael A. Keller/zefa), 30 (Nathan Benn), 31 (M. Thomsen/Zefa), 39 (H. Winkler/A.B./Zefa), 42 (James Robert Fuller).
Michael Courtney: 4, 5, 10, 14, 19, 24.
Miles Kelly Art Library: 6, 7, 8, 9, 20.
Science Photo Library: 11 (Alfred Pasieka), 12 (Prof. Peter Cull), 13 (Eye of Science), 15 (Simon Fraser), 16 (Astrid Kage), 17 (Mark Clarke), 18 (Prof. J. James), 21 (CNRI), 22 (John Walsh), 23 (John Greim), 25, 26 (John Bavosi), 27 (Manfred Kage), 28 (Ed Rescheke, Peter Arnold, Inc.), 29 (CNRI), 32 (Gusto), 33 (Sheila Terry), 36 (Ed Young / Agstock), 37 (Cordelia Molloy), 38 (John Heseltine), 40 (Dr. Gary Gaugler), 41 (Aaron Haupt), 44 (BSIP, Laurent), 45 (AJ Photo).
TopFoto: 34 (IMW), 35, 43 (IMW).

Note: The content of this book does not constitute medical advice. Consult appropriate health-care professionals in matters of personal health, medical care, and fitness.

Features included in this book:

- **FAQs** Each spread contains an FAQ panel. FAQ stands for Frequently Asked Question. The panels contain answers to typical questions that relate to the topic of the spread.

- **Glossary** There is a glossary of terms on pages 46–47. Terms defined in the glossary are *italicized* on their first appearance on any spread.

- **Additional resources** Books for further reading and recommended Web sites are listed on page 47. Because of the nature of the Internet, some Web site addresses may have changed since publication. The publisher has no responsibility for any such changes nor for the content of cited resources.

Contents

What is digestion?

When you put food into your mouth, it begins a journey through a set of organs inside your body that work together to break down the food so your body can use it. This system is called the digestive system. The journey takes more than a day. Along the way the food is broken down into small bits, or *molecules*, and substances that your body needs are extracted from it. This process of breaking down foods into *nutrients* that the *cells* of the body can absorb is called digestion.

Nutrients

The substances your body gets from digestion are called nutrients. Some nutrients are needed for the body to grow and repair itself. Some are needed for parts of the body, such as the brain, to work. Some provide the energy needed for walking, talking, and all the millions of chemical reactions that happen in the body. Energy is even needed to digest the food itself!

The main parts of the human digestive system.

mouth

esophagus

liver

stomach

pancreas

large intestine

small intestine

rectum

4

Digestive system parts

The digestive system starts at the mouth, where food goes in, and ends at the anus, where waste comes out. It is made up of a long tube called the alimentary canal, which is also called the digestive tract, or gut. Various organs and *glands*, such as the liver and salivary glands, are also part of the digestive system. As food passes through the alimentary canal, the food is broken down so that the useful substances it contains can be absorbed into the blood. Solid waste is passed out of the body as *feces*.

The urinary system

The digestive system gets rid of the waste parts of food that you eat. The urinary system is a separate system, but it also gets rid of waste—waste substances from the blood. The waste combines with water from the blood and makes *urine*. The urinary system is in the *abdomen*. It is made up of two kidneys that filter the blood; a pair of tubes through which urine passes from the kidneys to the urinary bladder; and a tube that carries the urine out of the body.

FAQ

Q. How long is the human digestive system?

A. The alimentary canal is about 30 feet (9 meters) long. The small intestine is the longest part. It measures about 22 feet (7 meters), and is coiled up to fit inside the body. Some parts of the alimentary canal are wider than others. The stomach is the widest part, and the small intestine is the narrowest.

kidneys
ureters
blood vessels
bladder
urethra

The main parts of the human urinary system.

Teeth and tongue

The digestive system starts in the mouth. There teeth and saliva begin the process of digestion even before food is swallowed. The teeth break pieces of food into smaller bits. The food is further broken down in the stomach and small intestine. Saliva begins to act chemically on the food, making it easier to swallow. The mouth is the only part of the digestive system that you control. The rest works completely automatically.

Teeth types

Adults have a total of 32 teeth, 16 each fixed firmly in the upper and lower jaws by long roots. There are eight incisors and four canines at the front of the mouth. These sharp front teeth are used for tearing and biting lumps off food.

FAQ

Q. What are teeth made of?

A. Teeth are made up of several layers. The outer, visible part is white enamel. Enamel is the hardest material in the body. Under the enamel is a layer called dentin. Dentin is harder than bone. In the middle is pulp, which contains blood vessels and *nerves*.

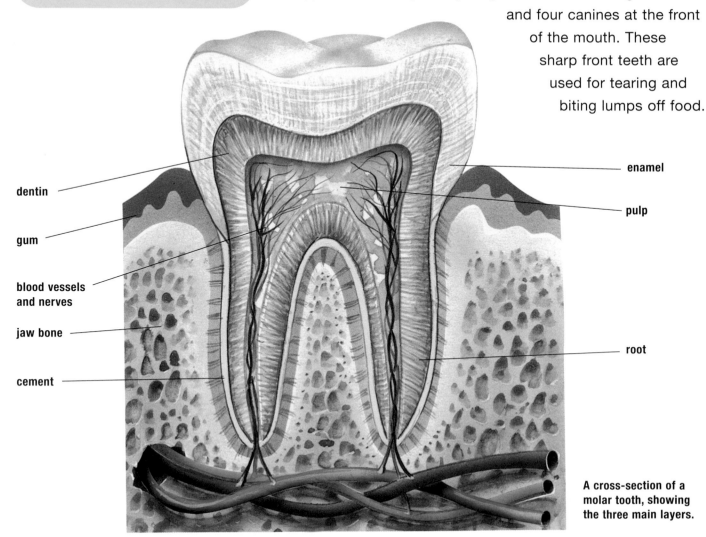

dentin

gum

blood vessels and nerves

jaw bone

cement

enamel

pulp

root

A cross-section of a molar tooth, showing the three main layers.

Next come eight premolars, which mash food. Farther back are 12 molars, which grind food. Young children have a set of 20 deciduous teeth, also called baby, milk, or primary teeth. These begin to be replaced by adult, or permanent, teeth when a child is about 6 or 7 years old.

Moving food around

The tongue is a *muscle* that moves food around in the mouth. It moves lumps of food backward so that the teeth can chew and grind them. The tongue gradually pushes chewed food into the back of the mouth, forming a lump of chewed food called a bolus. The tongue is covered with taste buds that detect different tastes. Taste is the first of the digestive system's defenses. If food tastes bad, you are less likely to swallow it.

Saliva

Saliva is a watery liquid made by salivary *glands* under the tongue and at the back of the mouth. Saliva is released through ducts into your mouth when you smell or taste food. Saliva helps chewing and swallowing by lubricating and softening the food. It also contains an *enzyme* called ptyalin that begins the chemical breakdown of starch in food. You produce about 2.5 pints (1.2 liters) of saliva per day!

rear of tongue

area sensitive to bitter tastes

area sensitive to salt tastes

area sensitive to sour tastes

area sensitive to salt tastes

area sensitive to salt tastes

area sensitive to sour tastes

area sensitive to salt tastes

area sensitive to sweet tastes

The top surface of the tongue. It is covered in tiny humps and hollows, making it feel rough.

From mouth to stomach

A bolus is a lump of chewed food mixed with saliva that is ready to be swallowed. When you swallow a bolus, *muscles* of the pharynx (a part of the throat) push the bolus into the next part of the alimentary canal, called the esophagus. This tube links the mouth to the stomach. The esophagus is also called the gullet.

Swallowing

Movements of the tongue push a bolus to the very back of the throat. Then the process of swallowing begins. The base of the tongue and muscles in the top of the throat push the bolus down into the esophagus. Once you start to swallow, all the muscles do the job automatically. It is important that food goes into the esophagus and not anywhere else. During swallowing the soft *palate* at the top of the back of the mouth closes to keep food from going into the nasal passages. And a flap called the epiglottis closes to keep food from going down the trachea (windpipe) into the lungs.

FAQ

Q. What makes me choke?

A. You choke when food fails to go into your esophagus and instead gets stuck in your trachea, the tube that carries air to your lungs. Your body makes you cough violently to try to get the food out. First aid for a person choking on food includes thrusting upward against the middle of the person's *abdomen*. This method is known as the Heimlich maneuver.

The swallowing process.

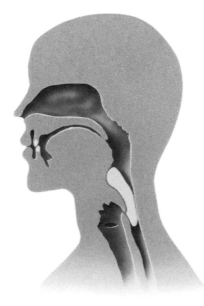

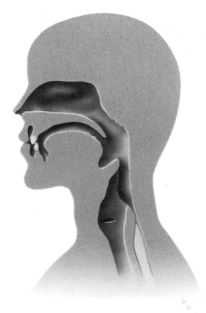

1. **Tongue pushes bolus (lump of chewed food) to back of mouth.**

2. **Epiglottis closes to stop food passing into trachea.**

3. **Muscles in esophagus push food towards stomach.**

Down the esophagus

The esophagus is lined with muscles that move food down into the stomach. The muscles automatically contract and relax, one after the other, forcing the bolus downward. This process is called *peristalsis* (see pages 10–11). It happens all along the alimentary canal. The esophagus is about 10 inches (25 centimeters) long. Food passes through it from mouth to stomach in about nine seconds.

In the lining of the esophagus are *glands* that produce *mucus*. This lubricates the esophagus, allowing food to slide down more easily. At the bottom of the esophagus is a muscular *valve* called a sphincter. It opens to let food into the stomach and then closes again.

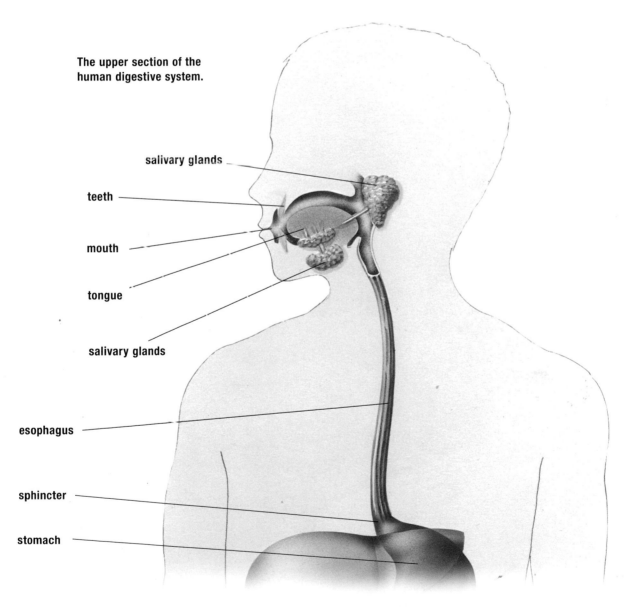

The upper section of the human digestive system.

salivary glands

teeth

mouth

tongue

salivary glands

esophagus

sphincter

stomach

Peristalsis

Because food moves downward through the digestive system, you might think it is moved by *gravity*. In fact, it is moved by actions of *muscles* in the walls of the alimentary canal. The muscles make the walls ripple, pushing the food along as if it were riding a wave. This process is called *peristalsis*. It happens from the top of the esophagus to the end of the large intestine.

Gut structure

The walls of the alimentary canal are similar all the way along. The outer layer protects it from damage. This layer is also slippery so that, for example, coils of intestines can safely lie against each other.

The inner layer—the mucosa—is the gut's lining. Between the inner and outer layers are two layers of muscle. In the inner muscle layer, *muscle fibers* go around the tube. In the outer muscle layer, muscle fibers go along the tube. The mucosa contains blood vessels that supply blood to the gut, and *nerves* that control the muscles.

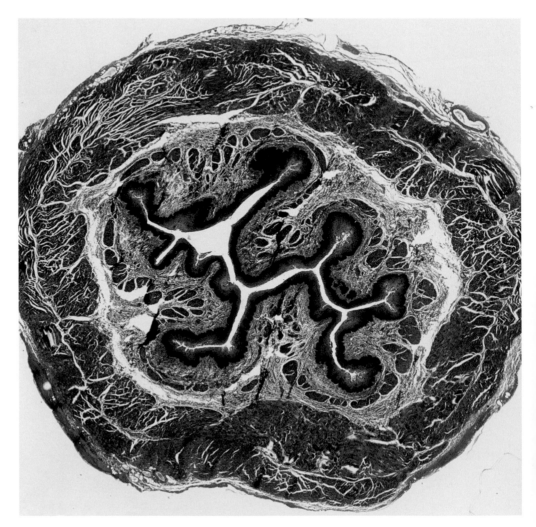

A cross-section of the esophagus, showing its two layers of muscle (the red area).

Muscle movements

When a bolus enters a part of the alimentary canal, that part of the tube stretches. Nerves detect this stretching and begin to make the muscles work. Muscles behind the bolus contract, squeezing the tube and pushing the bolus along. Then the muscles relax again. The moving bolus activates the next section of muscles, and the process is repeated. The result is a wave of muscle contractions, or tightenings, that move the bolus along. Peristalsis stops in a section of the alimentary canal when there is no food there to push along.

Digestive valves

There are several structures called sphincters in the alimentary canal. They are rings of muscle that work like *valves*. They close off sections of the canal from each other, keeping food from moving the wrong way.

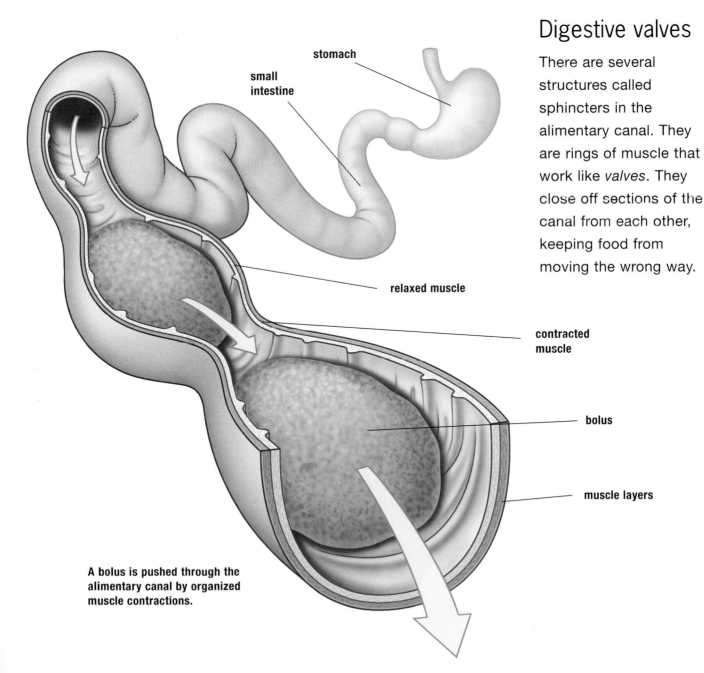

stomach

small intestine

relaxed muscle

contracted muscle

bolus

muscle layers

A bolus is pushed through the alimentary canal by organized muscle contractions.

The stomach

When food arrives at the bottom of the esophagus, it passes into the stomach. The stomach is made of strong *muscle* and is shaped like a bag or sack. It expands so that a meal of food can fit into it. An adult's stomach can hold a little over one quart (0.95 liter). The stomach's job is to act as a storage place for food and to start digesting the food with chemicals. After a meal, some food spends three to five hours in the stomach.

Stomach muscles

The stomach has four regions. Food from the esophagus goes into the top region, called the cardia. Then it gradually moves into the lower region, called the pylorus. Strong bands of muscles in the stomach walls move to churn the food. The stomach walls stretch to contain food until it is ready to be slowly released into the intestines.

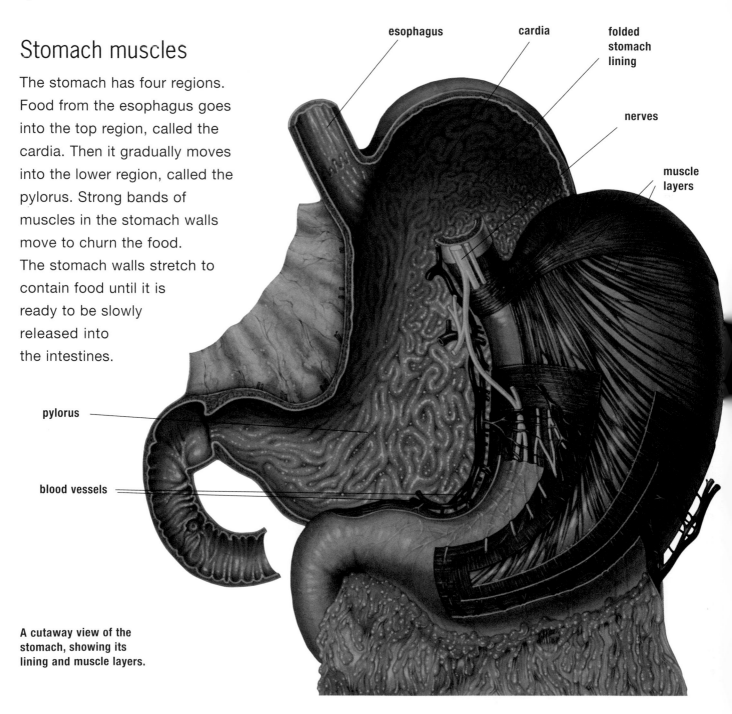

esophagus

cardia

folded stomach lining

nerves

muscle layers

pylorus

blood vessels

A cutaway view of the stomach, showing its lining and muscle layers.

Stomach acid

The stomach lining is full of tiny *glands*. These make liquids that are released into the stomach and combine into a fluid called gastric juice. The churning and squeezing of the stomach mixes the juice with the food. Gastric juice is a mixture of different chemicals, some of which make hydrochloric *acid*. It helps to break up the food, but also kills many harmful *microorganisms*, tiny living organisms such as bacteria, that the food may contain.

The stomach lining magnified 700 times. The lumps are individual cells of the lining.

Chemical workers

Other chemicals in the gastric juice begin breaking down some of the chemicals in the food. A chemical called pepsinogen in the juice combines with the stomach acid to make another chemical called pepsin. This breaks up chemicals in the food called *proteins* so the body can use them. Gastric juice also contains a chemical called intrinsic factor, which allows the body to use one of the *vitamins*, known as B12, found in food. The mixture of partly digested food and gastric juice is called chyme.

The stomach works automatically. It is controlled by *nerves* and chemicals called *hormones*. It releases chemicals and starts churning only when you smell and taste food and when nerves detect food in your mouth.

FAQ

Q. What protects the inside of my stomach from the burning action of the acid in it?

A. The hydrochloric acid in your stomach is a powerful chemical. If you put some of it in a test tube with a piece of metal, such as iron, it would eat away the metal. The lining of your stomach makes and coats itself with a substance called *mucus* that protects it from the acid.

The small intestine

The small intestine is the longest part of the digestive system. It is about 22 feet (7 meters) long but only about 1 inch (2.5 cm) in diameter. It is called the small intestine because it is narrow compared to the wider large intestine. The small intestine is coiled into the *abdomen*. In the small intestine, *nutrients* are absorbed into the blood. But more digestion happens in the duodenum first.

The duodenum

The duodenum is the first part of the small intestine. The duodenum is about 10 inches (25 centimeters) long. Small amounts of chyme from the stomach are squirted into the duodenum through a *valve* called the pyloric sphincter.

More digestive fluids are added to the chyme in the duodenum. These fluids are bile, which comes from a small pouch-shaped organ called the gallbladder, and pancreatic juice, which comes from the pancreas (see pages 16–17).

Bile breaks up *fat* into small droplets so that chemicals can break them up more easily. Pancreatic juice contains a mixture of digestive chemicals that break up *proteins*, *carbohydrates*,

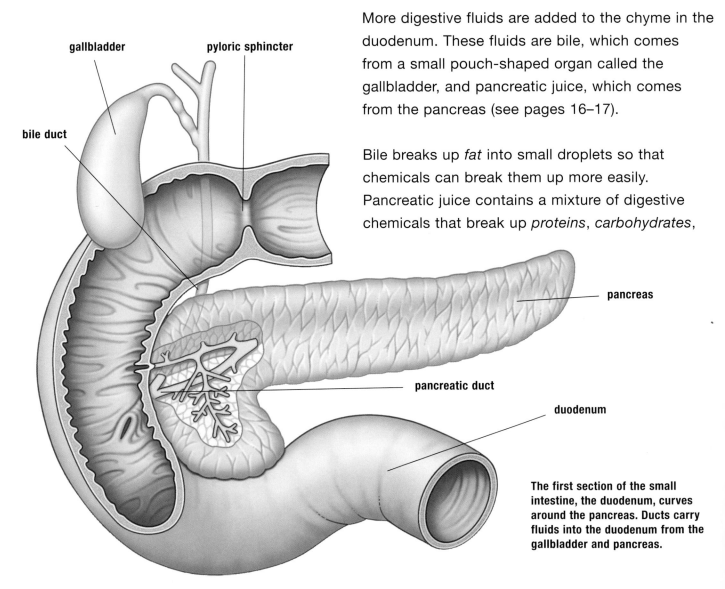

gallbladder

pyloric sphincter

bile duct

pancreas

pancreatic duct

duodenum

The first section of the small intestine, the duodenum, curves around the pancreas. Ducts carry fluids into the duodenum from the gallbladder and pancreas.

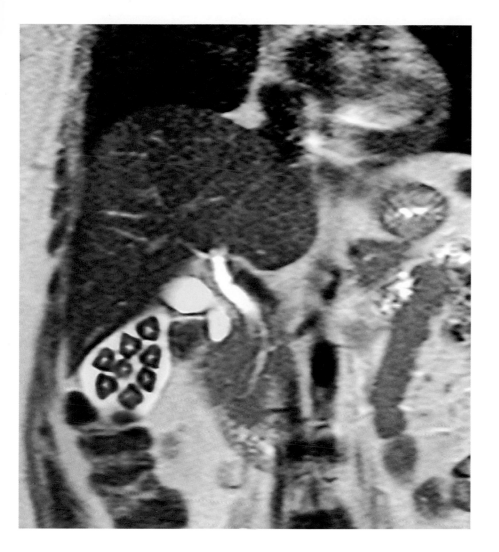

FAQ

Q. What are gallstones?

A. The gallbladder is a small bag-shaped organ that stores bile until it is needed. The bile is made by the liver (see pages 20–21). A gallstone is like a pebble that grows in the gallbladder. It is made from some of the chemicals in the bile. Gallstones can be painful, but they can be broken up by drugs or removed by surgery.

Gallstones show up as red lumps in this magnetic resonance imaging (MRI) scan of a patient's abdomen.

and fats. These chemicals can not work in the *acid* that comes from the stomach, so pancreatic juice also contains alkalis, substances that neutralize, or stop the effect of acid.

Absorbing nutrients

Such nutrients as sugars are made by digestion and absorbed into the blood and the *lymphatic system* through the lining of the small intestine. The surface of the lining is covered with millions of fingerlike tufts called villi. These give the lining a surface area larger than that of a tennis court. This huge surface area helps the body absorb more nutrients more quickly. The villi wave around to stir the contents of the intestine, which helps the nutrients to be absorbed. Food passes through the small intestine in about four or five hours.

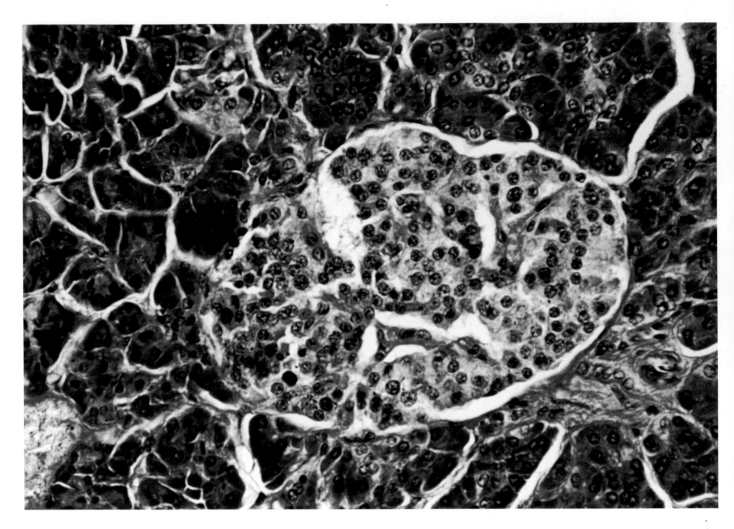

A magnified cross-section of the pancreas. Around the outside are cells that make pancreatic juice. The lighter area in the center is an islet of Langerhans that produces insulin.

The pancreas

The pancreas is a *gland* that plays an important part in digestion. The pancreas produces pancreatic juice, which flows into the duodenum. The pancreas is similar in shape to a carrot and about 6 to 8 inches (15 to 20 centimeters) long. The wide end is next to the duodenum. The pancreas also has another job: it controls the amount of sugar in the blood.

Making juice

Pancreatic juice is made inside the pancreas by bunches of *cells* called acini. The juice flows along narrow tubes that connect to the pancreatic duct. This duct joins the alimentary canal in the duodenum.

Pancreatic juice is a mixture of different digestive chemicals. The chemicals trypsin and chymotrypsin break up *proteins*, amylase breaks up starches, and lipase breaks up *fats*. Pancreatic juice also contains alkalis that neutralize stomach *acid*. The chemicals in pancreatic juice are powerful. They start to work only when they mix with the alkalis in the duodenum—otherwise they would digest the pancreas itself.

Insulin

The pancreas also makes a chemical called insulin. This is a *hormone* that controls the use by the body of sugar and other food for energy. Insulin is made in groups of cells called islets of Langerhans. There are about a million of them spread all through the pancreas. Insulin is not released into the pancreatic duct but directly into the blood that flows through the pancreas.

FAQ

Q. What is diabetes?

A. Diabetes is a disease that occurs when the body cannot use sugar properly. There are two types of diabetes. Type 1 diabetes happens when the pancreas cannot make enough insulin. In Type 2 diabetes there is usually enough insulin, but the body cannot use it. Diabetes causes sugar to build up in the blood, which can damage such organs as the eyes and kidneys. Some diabetes can be treated by controlling the intake of sugar or by injecting insulin.

A diabetic person using a blood sugar testing device. The results will tell her whether she needs an insulin injection.

Digestion chemicals

All the food you eat is made up of chemicals. The tiny particles that form these chemicals are called *molecules*. Molecules are made up of atoms joined together. Some molecules in food contain a few atoms, but most contain dozens or hundreds of thousands. Your body can not absorb most of these molecules because they are too large. The digestive system must break down the molecules into smaller molecules that the body can absorb.

Digestive enzymes

Breaking up molecules is a chemical change. It is done by chemicals called digestive *enzymes*. These work in the mouth, the stomach, and the small intestine, where they mix with food. Some enzymes are made by *cells* in the lining of the alimentary canal, and some are made by *glands* connected to the alimentary canal.

FAQ

Q. How does chewing help digestion?

A. The chewing teeth, and churning stomach, break food up into smaller and smaller pieces, but further action is needed to get food into a form the body can use. Breaking food up by chewing and churning allows digestive chemicals to work on finer particles of food, which makes digestion happen faster.

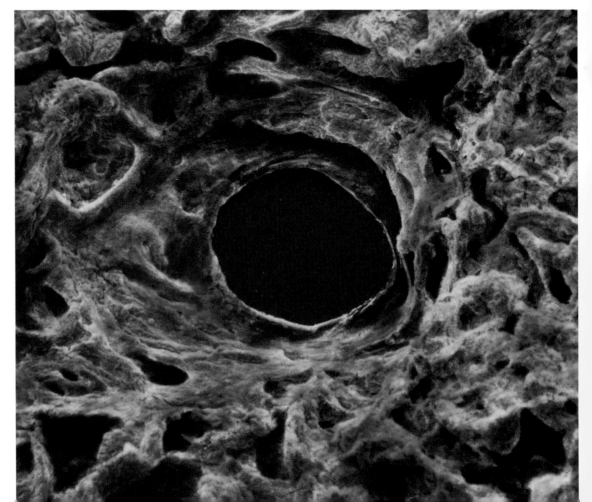

A magnified view of a stomach ulcer. An ulcer forms when the stomach lining itself is digested because mucus does not protect it.

Enzymes for food types

Different enzymes are designed to break down different chemicals in the foods you eat. The three main large molecules that need to be broken down are starches, *fats* (also called lipids), and *proteins*. You can find out on pages 30 to 33 which foods contain these chemicals.

Starch molecules are broken up by enzymes called ptyalin, contained in saliva, and amylase, contained in pancreatic juice. Ptyalin breaks the starch molecules into a simple sugar called maltose. Amylase breaks the maltose into even simpler molecules of a sugar called *glucose*.

Digestive enzymes break starch into maltose molecules and then into more simple glucose molecules.

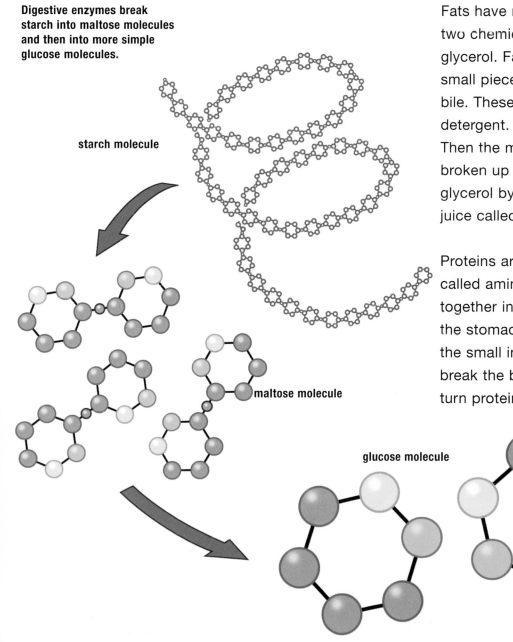

starch molecule

maltose molecule

glucose molecule

Fats have molecules made up of two chemicals called fatty *acids* and glycerol. Fats are broken first into small pieces by the chemicals in bile. These chemicals work like detergent. They pull fats apart. Then the molecules of fat are broken up into fatty acids and glycerol by an enzyme in pancreatic juice called lipase.

Proteins are made up of chemicals called amino acids that are joined together in long chains. Enzymes in the stomach, called pepsin, and in the small intestine, called trypsin, break the bonds of these chains to turn proteins into amino acids.

The liver

The liver is not part of the alimentary canal, but it is a vital part of the digestive system. The liver is like a chemical-processing factory. It takes chemicals that were absorbed in the small intestine and turns them into chemicals that the body can use and store for future use. The liver also makes bile, and it cleans the blood (see pages 22–23).

Shape and structure

The liver is almost the shape of a triangle. It is about 8 inches (20 centimeters) long and weighs about 3 pounds (1.4 kilograms). It has four parts, called lobes. Most livers contain up to a hundred thousand lobules. A lobule is made up of hundreds of liver *cells* situated around a central blood vessel that carries blood to and from the cells.

The human liver seen from the front, with two of its lobes visible. It is the body's largest internal organ.

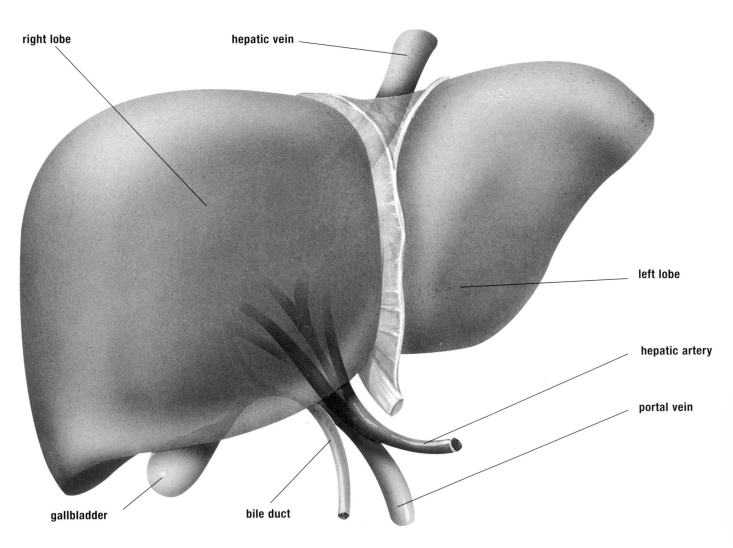

right lobe

hepatic vein

left lobe

hepatic artery

portal vein

gallbladder

bile duct

20

Blood reaches the liver through two blood vessels. The portal *vein* brings *nutrient*-rich blood straight from the intestines. The hepatic *artery* brings oxygen-rich blood from the heart. These two blood vessels divide into thousands of tiny blood vessels that pump blood into spaces in the liver called sinusoids. Liver cells take food and oxygen from the blood flowing through the sinusoids. Blood vessels from the lobules join up to form the hepatic vein, which carries blood away from the liver. The liver processes about 3 pints (1.4 liters) of blood every minute.

Digestive function

Liver cells process food *molecules* that come from the intestines. These cells break down some molecules into simpler ones and create nutrients from them. The liver stores some of the nutrients and puts others into the blood to be transported to other parts of the body. For example, the liver turns *glucose* into glycogen and stores it. Later the glycogen can be turned back into glucose and used for energy.

FAQ

Q. How much bile does the liver make?

A. Bile breaks up *fat* so that *enzymes* can get to the molecules of fat. The liver makes about 2 pints (1 liter) of bile every day. The bile is collected by tiny bile ducts. These join up to form the hepatic duct, which leads to the gallbladder, where the bile is stored.

A thin slice of liver seen through a microscope. It shows the center of a lobule. The central hole is a blood vessel.

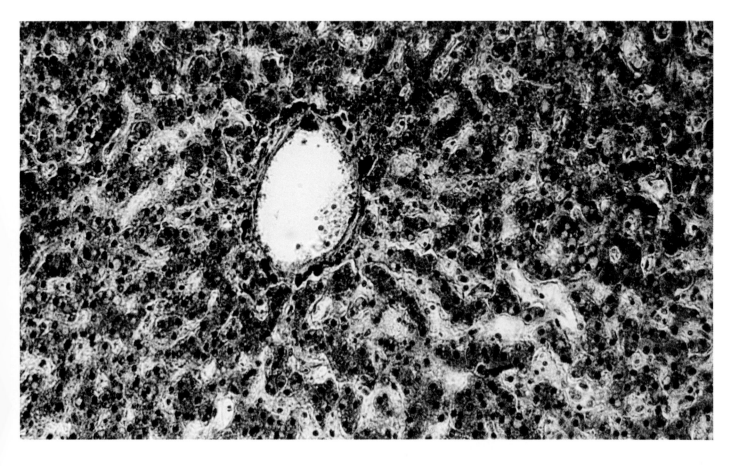

Cleaning the blood

As well as being part of the digestive system, the liver is a vital part of the *circulatory system*. This system is made up of the blood, the heart, and blood vessels. The blood carries *nutrients* and oxygen to all the *cells* in the body and carries carbon dioxide and other waste chemicals away from them. The liver removes some waste chemicals from the blood and also removes harmful chemicals called toxins.

Your liver breaks down harmful chemicals that you breathe in from the atmosphere, such as those pumped out by chemical factories.

Waste and toxins

Some of the chemicals that the liver removes from the blood are toxic substances from outside the body. These include poisons, alcohol, drugs, and pollutants breathed from the atmosphere, such as radon and sulfur dioxide. Other harmful chemicals are by-products of the body's own processes. The liver breaks them down into less harmful chemicals. This is done by hundreds of specialized *enzymes*. The less harmful chemicals are put back into the blood or the bile to be removed from the body.

Waste ammonia

Ammonia is an example of a waste product from the body's cells. It is made when *proteins* are broken down into, or built up from, amino *acids*. Ammonia is a toxic chemical that would cause harm if the body did not get rid of it. Ammonia from the cells goes into the blood. When it reaches the liver, the liver combines it with carbon dioxide, which is another waste product from cells.

This makes a less harmful chemical called urea, which the liver puts back into the blood. Urea is removed from the blood by the kidneys (see pages 26–27).

Waste routes

The less harmful chemicals made by the liver leave the body by different routes. Some chemicals that go back into the blood, such as urea, leave in *urine* made by the kidneys. Some go to the lungs and are breathed out. Some come out through the skin in sweat. Waste chemicals that go into bile leave the body as part of *feces*.

FAQ

Q. Can a damaged liver be repaired?

A. The liver is one of the few parts of the body that can grow back if it is damaged. This is called regeneration. For example, if half of a person's liver is removed because it is diseased, the remaining portion of the liver will grow back to its original size in a few weeks.

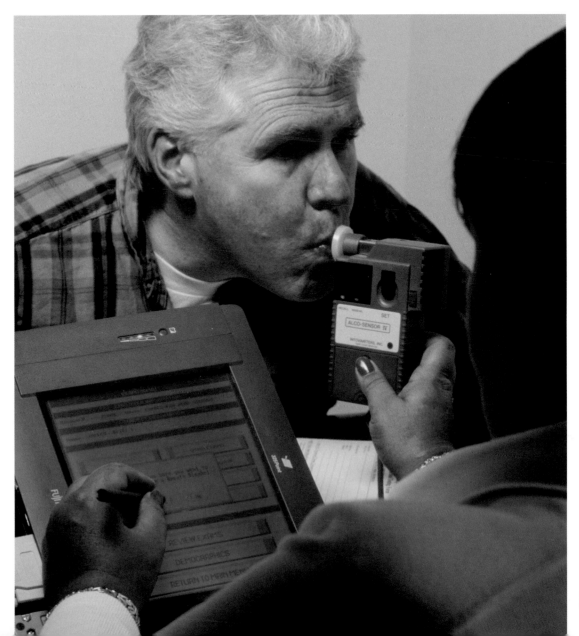

A breath test measures the level of alcohol in the blood. The liver breaks down alcohol, lowering the level.

The large intestine

The large intestine is the last part of the alimentary canal. The large intestine is much shorter and wider than the small intestine. Watery material from the small intestine enters the large intestine. The large intestine absorbs water and small amounts of *minerals* from this watery material. The water and minerals pass into the blood. This leaves a firm material called *feces*, which is passed out of the body.

Large intestine structure

The large intestine is made up of three main sections. They are the cecum, the colon, and the rectum. The cecum is short and wide. It joins the small and large intestines together. The colon is divided into four sections. They are the ascending colon, transverse colon, descending colon, and sigmoid colon. An adult's colon is about 5 feet (1.5 meters) long, and about 2.5 inches (6.3 centimeters) wide. The rectum is about 5 inches (12.5 centimeters) long.

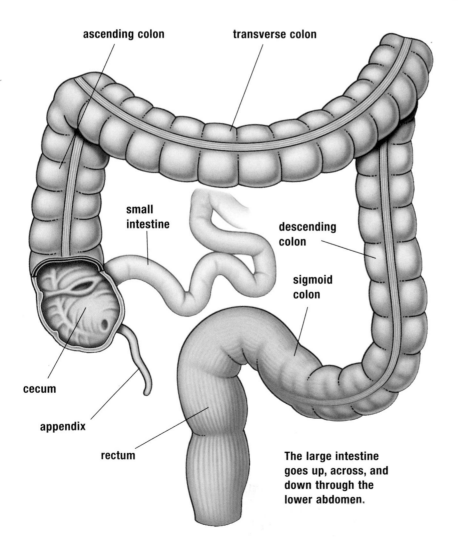

ascending colon

transverse colon

small intestine

descending colon

sigmoid colon

cecum

appendix

rectum

The large intestine goes up, across, and down through the lower abdomen.

Water and nutrients

A slushy mixture of water and undigested material enters the large intestine from the small intestine through a *valve*. By now, the small intestine has removed most *nutrients* from the food, but there are still some useful minerals left. These pass into the blood through the walls of the large intestine. Most of the water in the mixture also is absorbed. About 4 pints (2 liters) enter the large intestine every day, and about 3.6 pints (1.8 liters) of it are absorbed.

After the minerals and water have been removed, the material left over is called *feces*. About two-thirds of it is water and about one-third is solid material, made up mostly of undigested plant *fiber*, bacteria, bile, *mucus*, and old *cells* from the lining of the alimentary canal. Feces are stored in the rectum until you go to toilet, when they are released through the anus. Always thoroughly wash your hands with soap and water after going to the toilet.

Bacteria in the gut

Harmless bacteria live in every part of your alimentary canal, from your mouth to your large intestine. Millions of bacteria live in the large intestine and are contained in feces. Many are friendly bacteria that help with digestion.

FAQ

Q. What does the appendix do?

A. The answer is probably nothing at all. The appendix is a small tube a few inches long that extends from the cecum. Scientists do not really know why it is there. Feces trapped in the appendix can cause infection and serious, painful swelling called appendicitis.

An X-ray of the first part of the large intestine. The fingerlike object on the left is the appendix.

The kidneys

The kidneys are the first part of the urinary system. The urinary system has two main jobs. It removes waste chemicals from the body, and it removes water if there is too much of it in the body. The kidneys remove waste and water from the blood using tiny structures that work like filters. The other parts of the urinary system drain the excess water and waste from the body (see pages 28–29). You have one kidney on each side of your body. They look like huge purplish-brown beans. Each one is about 4.5 inches (11.4 centimeters) long.

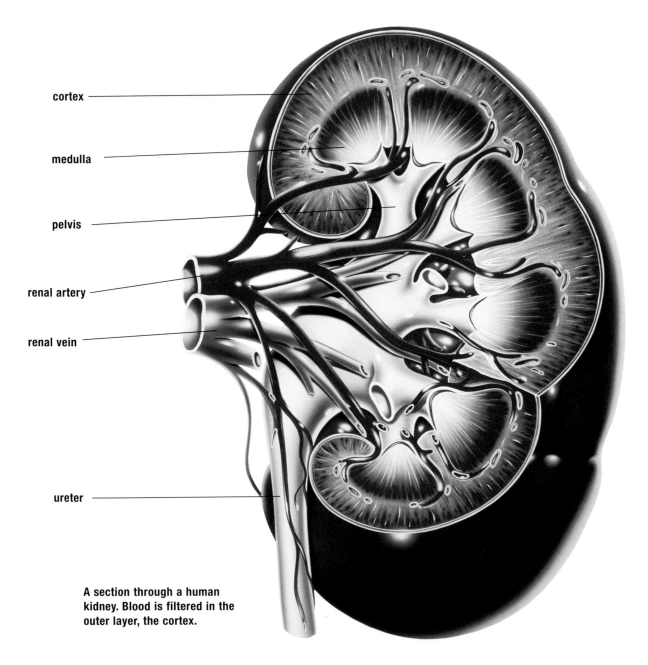

cortex

medulla

pelvis

renal artery

renal vein

ureter

A section through a human kidney. Blood is filtered in the outer layer, the cortex.

Kidney function

Blood flows to the kidneys through the renal *artery* and then flows away again through the renal *vein*. The kidneys filter waste chemicals from the plasma (the watery part of blood) as it passes through them. A kidney has three layers. From inside to outside, these are the pelvis, the medulla, and the cortex. The cortex of each kidney contains more than a million tiny blood-filtering structures called nephrons.

Blood filters

In each nephron is a tiny bunch of blood vessels inside a case called a Bowman's capsule. There most of the water and other chemicals are filtered from the blood. They flow into a long, twisting tube that leads away from the capsule. The tube is surrounded by blood vessels that lead to the renal vein. Useful chemicals and nearly all the water in the tube pass through the walls of the tube and go back into blood vessels, which join up to form the renal vein.

Waste chemicals stay in the tube. Tubes from all the nephrons go into the medulla. They join together at the pelvis of the kidney and then narrow to form a single tube called a ureter. The water and waste materials are called *urine*. An adult produces about 1 to 2 quarts (0.95 to 1.9 liters) of urine per day.

A magnified cross-section of part of a kidney. The large white shape is a Bowman's capsule. Tiny blood vessels are bundled inside it.

FAQ

Q. What is kidney dialysis?

A. Sometimes a person's kidneys stop cleaning blood properly. This is called renal failure. It is serious because it allows poisonous waste materials to build up in the blood. One treatment for renal failure is called kidney dialysis. A dialysis machine takes blood from an artery in a patient's arm, cleans it, and then pumps it back into a vein in the patient's arm.

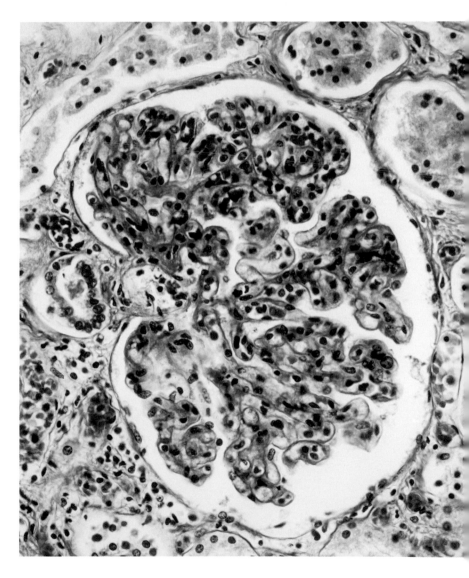

The urinary tract

Urine from the kidneys flows out of the body along a system of tubes called the urinary tract. The tract is made up of two ureters (one from each kidney), the bladder, and the urethra. The ureters carry *urine* to the bladder, the bladder stores the urine, and the urethra carries it from the bladder out of the body.

Ureters

The ureters are tubes about 12 inches (30 centimeters) long. They have *muscles* in their walls that squeeze urine along to the bladder in a way similar to *peristalsis* in the alimentary canal. The ureters go from the kidneys, down the back of the *abdomen*, and into the top of the bladder. Tiny folds at the bottom of the ureters help keep urine from going back up the ureters to the kidneys.

A cross-section of a ureter viewed through a microscope. You can see the central channel through which urine flows. The outer two layers are muscle.

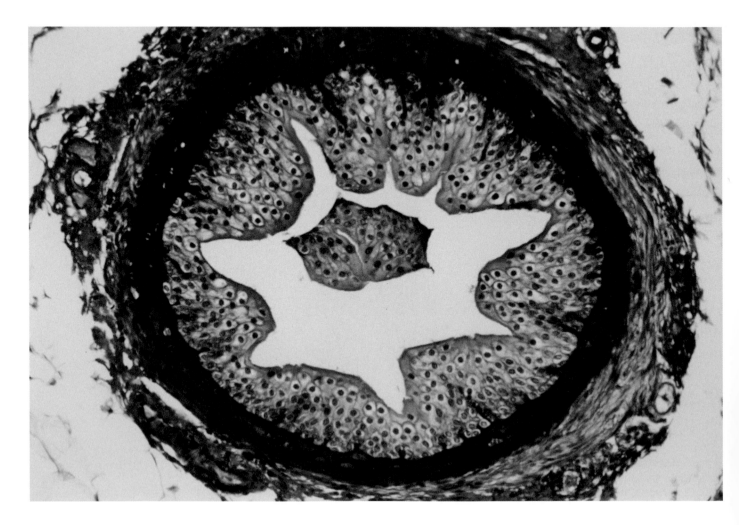

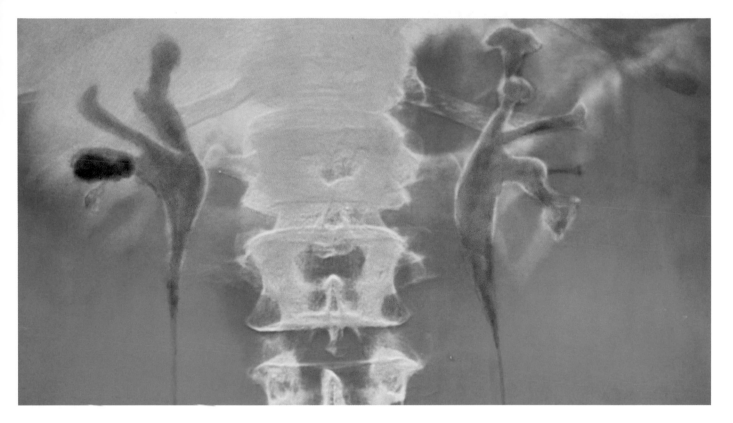

Bladder and urethra

The urinary bladder is a bag-shaped organ made up of *muscle fibers* that stores urine. When the bladder is empty, it is small and wrinkled. It expands as urine trickles in from the ureters. It can hold more than a pint (half a liter) of urine. The urethra is a tube that leads from the bottom of the bladder to the outside of the body.

Going to the toilet

When your bladder is about half full, you begin to feel that you want to go to the toilet. When you do go, you relax a ring of muscles called the urethral sphincter that surrounds the opening from the bladder to the urethra. Then, the muscles in the bladder automatically squeeze urine out through the urethra. Children learn to control their bladders when they are about two or three. Always thoroughly wash your hands with soap and water after going to the toilet.

A specialized X-ray shows fluid draining from the kidneys into the ureters. The red patch on the left is a kidney stone.

FAQ

Q. What are kidney stones?

A. Sometimes hard lumps grow in the kidneys. These lumps are called kidney stones. They are made from chemicals in urine. Large stones can cause pain as they move along the ureters, and they can block the ureters completely, causing infection. Kidney stones can be washed out by drinking lots of water, broken up with sound waves, or removed by surgery.

Food for growth

The food you eat contains a huge range of different chemicals. However, only a few dozen of these chemicals are absolutely needed to keep us healthy. These few dozen are the *nutrients*. These nutrients come from six kinds of substances found in food. They are *proteins* (see below), *fats* and *carbohydrates* (see pages 32–33), *vitamins* and *minerals* (see pages 36–37), and water. Water is vital for life.

Proteins

You need to eat proteins so that your body can grow and repair itself and so that its systems can work properly. Proteins are one of the most important building blocks of the body. They make up a large part of each *cell* in the body, so your *muscles* and skin, for example, are mostly proteins. Some proteins control the chemical reactions that make your

Meat, eggs, cheese, and nuts all contain high amounts of protein.

body work. For example, the *enzymes* made by the digestive system are proteins. Foods that contain proteins include fish, meat, nuts, eggs, cheese and other dairy products, and some vegetables, including peas.

Amino acids

Proteins are made up of particles called *molecules*. A protein molecule is made up of smaller molecules joined together. These smaller molecules are called amino *acids*. The human body uses only 20 different types of amino acids, but they are combined together in different amounts and in different mixtures to make the thousands of different proteins that make up the body. Proteins in food are broken up into amino acids by enzymes in the digestive system. Cells in the liver and other organs build the amino acids into new proteins for the body. Sometimes, amino acids instead can be turned into energy for the body.

You can survive only a few days without drinking water.

FAQ

Q. How much water should I drink?

A. About two-thirds of your body is made up of water, and water is vital for your body to work properly. You lose water all the time through the elimination of body wastes and sweating. You must take in water to make up for these losses. An adult needs to take in about 2.5 quarts (2.4 liters) of water a day in the form of beverages or water in food.

Food for energy

Your body uses energy all the time. Movements such as walking, running, and jumping all require energy. Your body also needs energy when you are sitting still and even when you are asleep. Energy is needed for thinking and for such processes as digestion and circulation. It also is needed for replacing old *cells* and repairing damage. All this energy comes from *carbohydrates*, *fats*, and *proteins* in the food you eat. These all are broken down into simpler substances by the digestive system. The simpler substances are either broken down to obtain energy, or combined to create substances that can be used for energy when needed. Energy is moved to different parts of the body as *glucose*.

Carbohydrates

Carbohydrates are made up of the chemical elements carbon, hydrogen, and oxygen. In a well-balanced diet, carbohydrates should give you about half the energy you need. An important source of energy is a carbohydrate called starch. It is found in potatoes, rice, and cereals (such as wheat, oats, and barley), and also in foods made from cereals, such as pasta and corn flakes. Starch is made up of *molecules* of sugar joined together. Digestive *enzymes* break up the starch into glucose, which the body can absorb. Sugars in food are also carbohydrates. They are broken down into glucose, too.

Potatoes, bread, rice, and pasta are all rich in carbohydrates.

Butter, sunflower oil, and olive oil are all rich in fats.

Fats

Fats (which are also called lipids) are chemicals found in the fatty parts of animals and in vegetable oils. Fats are found in fatty red meats, dairy products (milk, butter, and cheese), and nuts and seeds. Vegetable cooking oils, such as olive oil, and spreads, such as sunflower margarine, contain oils from nuts and seeds, so they also contain fats. Fats are broken down into chemicals called fatty *acids* by the digestive system. These are broken down by the liver to make glucose.

FAQ

Q. Where is energy stored?

A. Sugars and fatty acids are absorbed by the body in the hours after a meal. Some sugars and fatty acids are used for energy right away, but others are stored so that you have a steady supply of energy. The liver turns the sugar glucose into glycogen, which is stored in the liver and in cells around the body. The liver turns the stored glycogen back into glucose when the level of sugar in the blood becomes low. The liver stores fatty acids in the form of fat.

33

Measuring food energy

Different foods provide your body with different amounts of energy. This is because they contain different amounts of *carbohydrates* and *fats*. For example, pasta contains lots of carbohydrates, and so it is a high-energy food. Carrots contain a small amount of carbohydrates and almost no fats, so they provide little energy (however, they do contain important *vitamins*). The amount of energy in packaged foods is usually printed on the package label, so you can see how much energy is in them.

Calories

The energy in food is measured in units called kilocalories. One kilocalorie is equal to 1,000 calories. A calorie is the amount of energy needed to raise one gram of water one Celsius degree. Kilocalories often simply are referred to as "calories." Heat energy also can be measured in units called joules. One kilocalorie equals 4,184 joules, or 4.184 kilojoules.

Nutrition Facts

Serving Size   1 carton (250 mL)

Amount per serving

Calories 150   Calories from Fat 30

	% Daily Value*
Total Fat 3g	4%
Saturated Fat 0g	0%
Cholesterol 0mg	0%
Sodium 95mg	4%
Potassium 310mg	8%
Total Carbohydrate 24g	8%
Sugars 15g	
Protein 6g	12%
Calcium 6% •	Iron 4%
Thiamin (B1)	8%
Riboflavin (B2) 4% • Niacin (B3) 6%	
Pantothenic Acid (B5)	8%
Pyridoxine Hydrochloride (B6) 8%	
Folate (B9) 10% • Biotin (Vit H) 2%	
Phosphorus 10% • Magnesium 10%	
Zinc 4% •	Copper 9%

Not a significant source of cholesterol, dietary fiber, Vit. A & C. * % Daily Values are based on a 2,000 calorie per day diet.

INGREDIENTS: Purified Water, Organic Soybeans, Naturally Malted Corn and Barley Extract, Vanilla Extract, Kombu Seaweed, Sea Salt

The nutrition panel on the side of a food package. The number of calories is shown at the top.

The energy in foods

Beans, green, canned, 1 cup	25c
Carrot, grated, raw, 1 cup	45c
Slice of bread and butter	100c
Pizza, cheese, 15-inch diameter, $\frac{1}{8}$ portion	290c
Pork chop, pan fried	335c
Pie, apple, $\frac{1}{6}$ portion	405c
Chicken potpie, 1 pie	545c

How much energy do we need?

The amount of energy a person needs to take in depends on the person's sex, age, height, weight, and usual level of activity. For example, adults who do manual work, such as building construction, generally need more energy than adults who work at a desk.

A few hours before running a race, long-distance runners often eat foods that contain lots of carbohydrates. Their digestive system turns the carbohydrates into *glucose*, which is stored in their liver as glycogen. The glycogen is converted, or changed, to glucose for energy as the runners need it during the race.

If you take in more calories than your body burns, most of the excess calories will be stored in your body as fat. If you eat fewer calories than your body burns, your body will burn stored fat for energy.

FAQ

Q. How long would it take to "walk off" a slice of cake?

A. It would take a little more than an hour of walking at a moderate pace to burn all the calories in a slice of cake with frosting. It would take almost three-quarters of an hour of walking at a rapid pace to burn those calories.

Athletes need an above average amount of carbohydrates to give them the energy to train and compete.

Vitamins and minerals

Vitamins and *minerals* are substances that your body needs in order to work properly. A few vitamins are formed in the body, but other vitamins and all minerals must be obtained from food. Vitamins and minerals, unlike *proteins*, *carbohydrates*, and *fats*, do not need to be broken up in the digestive system before they can be absorbed. Vitamins and minerals often are called micronutrients because you need them in only tiny amounts—you need to eat far less of them than you do proteins, carbohydrates, and fats. Vitamins and minerals do not contain any energy at all.

Fresh fruits and vegetables contain a wide range of vitamins and minerals.

Vitamins

Vitamins are needed for growing and repairing parts of the body, and they take part in many chemical processes in the body. Scientists have discovered about 20 different vitamins, which they have named with letters and numbers.

FAQ

Q. Why should we eat fruits and vegetables?

A. Not eating enough of a certain vitamin can cause diseases. For example, a disease called scurvy is caused by not consuming enough vitamin C. Hundreds of years ago scurvy was a common disease on long sea voyages because sailors did not have enough fresh fruit and vegetables to eat.

Each vitamin does a different job in the body. For example, vitamin A is needed to maintain the skin, eyes, bones, and teeth, and vitamin K is needed to make blood clot properly. Some vitamins also have chemical names. For example, vitamin C is also called ascorbic *acid*.

Some common vitamins and foods that contain them

Vitamin	Food
A	butter, fish liver oil, carrots
B1	whole grains, organ meats, nuts, most vegetables
C	oranges, lemons, tomatoes
D	fish, fortified milk
E	almost all foods
K	leafy vegetables

Minerals

Minerals include such elements as calcium, iron, and iodine. They are absorbed into the blood from the intestines. Different minerals are needed for different body processes. For example, iron is needed for red blood *cells* to carry oxygen, and sodium helps regulate water in the body's cells.

Major minerals are minerals that we need in relatively large amounts. They include sodium, calcium, magnesium, potassium, phosphorus, chlorine, and sulfur. Trace minerals (also called trace elements) are needed in smaller amounts. They include copper, iron, and zinc.

Pregnant women often take pills containing iron (a mineral) and folic acid (a vitamin). These nutrients help their unborn babies to grow.

A balanced diet

Your diet is all the food and liquid that you consume. A diet that provides you with all the *nutrients* you need without giving you too much of any of them is known as a balanced diet. A diet that leaves out an important nutrient, such as a *vitamin*, can cause health problems. A diet that includes too many *carbohydrates* or *fats* can cause health problems, too.

Eating a balanced diet is easy. It simply means eating a good mixture of foods, including foods that contain carbohydrates, *fiber*, and *protein*. It also means not eating too many fatty or sugary foods.

An example of a balanced meal. It contains proteins, fats, carbohydrates, vitamins, and fiber.

Recommended dietary allowances

Scientists have worked out how much of each nutrient we need every day in order to stay healthy. These amounts are called recommended dietary allowances (RDAs). They are measured in grams, milligrams, or micrograms. The amount of different nutrients in different types of food usually is shown on food packages. This allows us to work out how much of each nutrient we are eating. Most foods contain a mixture of different types of nutrients.

FAQ

Q. Why should infants and children drink milk?

A. Infants and children need to drink milk because it has almost all the nourishing substances humans need for growth and good health. For example, milk is the most important food source of calcium, which is needed for healthy development of bones and teeth.

Good and bad foods

Eating a lot of foods that contain fats and carbohydrates, such as fried foods and sugary foods, can be unhealthy. If a person does not use up the energy he or she eats as food, the extra energy is stored as fat in that person's body. This can make the person overweight and cause health problems, such as heart disease. There is nothing wrong with eating these foods in small amounts, as long as they are balanced with more healthy foods.

Milk is the most important source of the mineral calcium for young people. It also contains energy-giving fat.

Food poisoning

Sometimes harmful microorganisms invade the digestive system. This can happen when you eat food that has bacteria growing on it. Some bacteria grow in food and produce toxins (poisons), which can cause illness. Some *microorganisms*, including bacteria, viruses, or parasites, can enter the body through food and cause infection when they multiply. Such an infection may result in an upset stomach, with pain, vomiting, or diarrhea (frequent elimination of watery *feces*).

Similar illnesses are caused by eating poisonous foods, such as toadstools or foods with poisonous chemicals in them. You can avoid food poisoning by eating only food that you are sure has been properly stored and prepared.

Bacteria for food poisoning

Salmonella is the name of a kind of bacteria that causes food poisoning. Salmonella is found in beef, poultry and eggs, and dairy products. It can be spread by allowing clean food to touch contaminated surfaces. We protect ourselves from salmonella by *pasteurizing* milk and by handling food properly.

Washing hands removes bacteria that could be transferred to food before it is eaten.

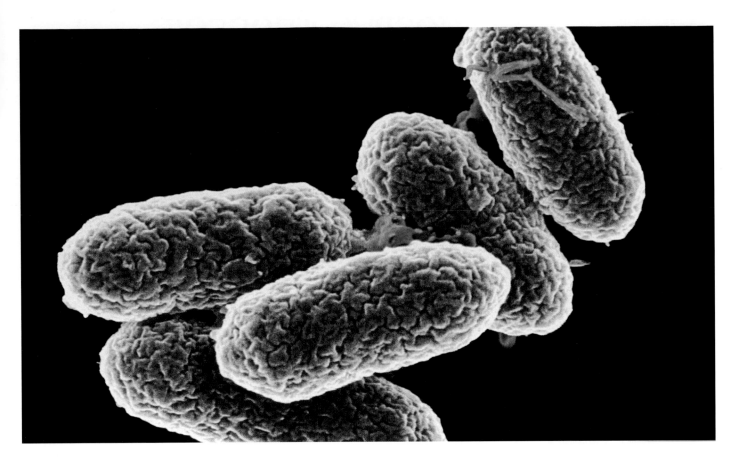

Another common cause of food-poisoning is bacteria called clostridium. It grows on meat that is cooked and then allowed to cool slowly instead of being put in the refrigerator. One form of clostridium causes a severe form of food poisoning called botulism, which can be fatal. Most cases of food poisoning can be cured by not eating for a day and drinking plenty of clear fluids.

Infection and *inflammation* of the stomach and intestines is called gastroenteritis. It is often caused by food poisoning. It causes stomach pains, vomiting, and diarrhea. Gastroenteritis may occur in groups of people who ate the same contaminated food.

Salmonella bacteria magnified 300,000 times. They are a common cause of food poisoning.

Vomiting

Your body empties poisoned food from your stomach by vomiting. You cannot prevent it. Vomiting occurs when the brain signals the diaphragm and abdominal *muscles* to squeeze the stomach. The stomach contents then are forced up and out through the esophagus.

Digestive illnesses

Survivors of the tsunami of December 26, 2004, in Aceh, Indonesia. The only available water for drinking and cooking is contaminated with sewage.

Serious infections of the digestive tract are widespread in some areas of the world. These areas are normally where people do not have access to clean drinking water or the *sanitation* is poor. But these illnesses also can happen in developed countries if sewage systems are flooded during natural disasters, such as hurricanes.

Serious diseases of the digestive tract include dysentery, typhoid fever, and cholera. These infections are caused by harmful *microorganisms* in contaminated water or food. Excessive loss of body fluid because of diarrhea caused by these diseases can be fatal.

Problems of diarrhea

When a person has diarrhea, water and *minerals* are lost in frequent bowel movements before they can be absorbed by the body. This is a serious problem because such organs as the brain and kidneys cannot work without water and certain minerals.

The treatment for diarrhea is called oral rehydration. The patient drinks water mixed with sugar for energy and salts that contain minerals. Without rehydration a person with severe diarrhea can die in only a few days. Worldwide, diarrhea caused by dysentery, cholera, or typhoid fever is a major cause of childhood deaths.

Dysentery

Dysentery results in *inflammation* of the large intestine. It causes severe abdominal pain and diarrhea with blood in it. It is caused by bacteria or other tiny organisms in drinking water or on food. Dysentery spreads very quickly and easily. It is treated with *antibiotics* and rehydration.

Indian children being given oral rehydration salts to counteract the effects of severe diarrhea.

Cholera

Cholera is an infection of the intestines that is caused by bacteria called Vibrio cholerae. The bacteria release a toxin that causes severe diarrhea. Cholera is often caused by contamination of drinking water by sewage. It is common in tropical areas of the world, especially in Asia.

Typhoid fever

Typhoid fever is an infection of the intestines caused by one type of salmonella bacteria. It causes headaches and fever as well as diarrhea. It is spread by poor sanitation and hygiene.

FAQ

Q. What spreads diseases?

A. Most diseases of the digestive tract are spread by water. The bacteria that cause the diseases are in *feces*. Sometimes feces end up in rivers or other sources that are used to supply drinking water. The diseases can be avoided by boiling water before drinking it. The high temperature of boiling kills the bacteria.

Healthy digestion

You have to look after your digestive system to keep it working properly. You can do this by avoiding foods that will upset your stomach or intestines or are difficult to digest. It also means looking after the only parts of your digestive system that you can touch—your teeth.

Indigestion causes a painful burning sensation in the chest as stomach acid rises into the esophagus.

Indigestion

Pains in the stomach and chest often happen because the stomach cannot digest food properly. This is called *acid* indigestion or dyspepsia. It often causes heartburn. This is a burning feeling in the chest that happens when acid from the stomach gets into the esophagus.

Indigestion is normally caused by eating too much food too quickly, especially greasy or spicy food. Exercising too soon after eating can also cause indigestion. Occasional indigestion can be relieved by taking indigestion tablets. These contain alkalis, which neutralize *acid*.

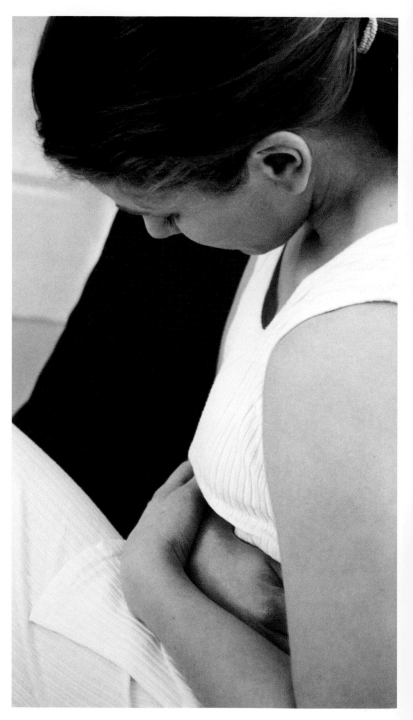

FAQs

Q. **What is a hiccup?**

A. A hiccup is a quick, involuntary intake of air that happens when a muscle called the diaphragm contracts sharply. The "hik" sound that we hear results from air passing through the voice box. Hiccups can happen if you irritate your stomach by eating too much food.

Eating roughage

Roughage is made up of plant *fibers* in vegetables, fruits, and cereals and in seeds from plants such as lentils. You cannot digest roughage, but it is important for your digestive system. It gives *feces* some bulk. This helps give the *muscles* in the intestine walls something to push against.

Not eating enough roughage can cause constipation. This is when feces stay in the intestines for longer than normal. More water is absorbed from the feces by the body, so the waste becomes dry and hard. Scientists think that not eating enough roughage also may make colon cancer more likely.

Tooth care

Looking after your teeth is important because chewing food helps digestion in the stomach and intestines. Brushing your teeth after meals removes food particles from the teeth. Bacteria that feed on food particles produce acid that rots the teeth. Looking after your gums is just as important because they support the teeth. You also can take care of your teeth by avoiding too many sugary foods and drinks, as well as by going to the dentist regularly.

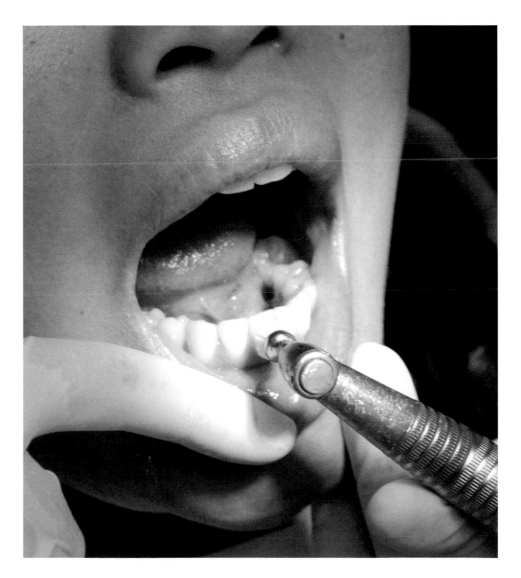

Regular checkups at the dentist enable repairs to be carried out before teeth become badly damaged.

Glossary

abdomen The lower part of the body, underneath the diaphragm. It contains all the digestive organs.

acid A chemical that eats away at some materials, such as metals.

antibiotic A drug that kills bacteria.

artery A blood vessel that carries blood from the heart to a part of the body. For example, the renal artery carries blood from the heart to the kidneys.

carbohydrate One of the main substances in food that the digestive system breaks down for energy.

cell The basic building block of the body. Your body contains hundreds of different types of cells, such as blood cells, skin cells, and nerve cells.

circulatory system The system that carries blood to all parts of the body. It is made up of the heart and blood vessels.

enzyme A substance that helps chemical changes happen in the body. Digestive enzymes help break down food into chemicals that the body can absorb.

fat One of the main substances in food that the digestive system breaks down for energy.

feces A mixture of undigested substances from food, water, bacteria, and other material. Feces are formed in the large intestine and pass out of the body.

fiber Edible plant material that normally passes undigested through the body.

gland An organ in the body that makes chemicals that the body needs, such as enzymes and hormones.

glucose A type of sugar that the body uses as a source of energy.

gravity The force that pulls everything on the earth downward.

hormone A chemical that controls how a part of the body works.

inflammation Swelling and redness that happens at a place infected by harmful bacteria.

lymphatic system A system of vessels that drain fluid from the body's cells into the blood.

microorganism A living thing that is too small to see with the naked eye but can be seen with a microscope.

mineral Any simple chemical found in food that is vital for the body to function properly.

molecule A tiny particle that makes up many materials. Molecules are made up of atoms joined together.

mucus A slimy fluid in the alimentary canal that helps food slide easily through.

muscle A type of body tissue that can contract under control of nerves.

muscle fiber A long, thin fiber inside a muscle. Muscle fibers are the parts of the muscle that contract.

nerve A long, thin bundle of cells that carries tiny electric signals in the body to control muscles, organs, and other body parts.

nutrient A chemical in food that the body needs in order to work properly.

palate The roof of the mouth.

pasteurization Treating food to kill bacteria in it. Milk is pasteurized by heating it and then quickly cooling it.

peristalsis The process that pushes food along the alimentary canal using muscles in the walls of the canal.

protein A type of chemical in food that the digestive system breaks down to allow the body to grow and repair itself.

sanitation A system of pipes that carries away waste water and sewage from a house.

urine A mixture of water and waste produced by the kidneys.

valve A device or structure that controls the flow of liquid, for example, in a pipe. It can also be closed to keep the liquid from flowing.

vein A blood vessel that carries blood from a part of the body back to the heart. For example, the renal vein carries blood from the kidneys to the heart.

vitamin A chemical that is needed to make certain body processes work properly.

Additional resources

Books

Ballard, Carol. *Exploring the Human Body: The Stomach and Digestion.* San Diego, CA: KidHaven Press, 2005.

Parker, Steve. *Human Body: Food and Digestion.* New York: Franklin Watts, 1990.

Whitfield, Philip, ed. *The Human Body Explained: A Guide to Understanding the Incredible Living Machine.* New York: Henry Holt, 1995.

Web sites

http://kidshealth.org/kid/body/digest_noSW.html
An entertaining guide to the digestive system and other body parts.

http://www.harcourtschool.com/activity/digest/
An interactive diagram to how the digestive system processes different foods.

http://kidshealth.org/kid/stay_healthy/food/pyramid.html
A friendly and simple guide to a balanced diet.

http://www.niddk.nih.gov
Home page of the National Institute of Diabetes and Digestive and Kidney Disorders.

http://www.niddk.nih.gov/health/digest/pubs/digesyst/newdiges.htm
National Digestive Diseases Information Clearinghouse site on the digestive system.

Index

Page numbers in **bold** refer to illustrations.